Your Digital Footprint

And

Password Protection Requirements

return to Smashwords.com and purchase your own copy. Thank you for respecting the hard work of this author.

Thank you for your support of the author's rights.

Book Description

At present, it is quite common to fall prey to online identity thieves if you are not being careful. If you think about it, there are a lot of people who have already suffered consequences by having easily accessible online accounts. Because of this, they had to face a lot of headaches like dealing with the police and fixing their credit card account mishaps. Some even had their online and offline reputations shredded to bits without them having the slightest idea it was going to happen. Experts advise you to come up with strong passwords to prevent this. Furthermore, you have to make each of your account passwords unique enough to decrease the risks of having your passwords stolen.

It is quite understandable you cannot remember every single password for each of your accounts. In fact, most of the users who have already created numerous passwords for more than five accounts confess that they too cannot remember all of the passwords that they initially generated. However, this does not mean that these codes are not unique and strong. They and you simply have come up with ways to help recall passwords when time to make the log-in input.

Actually, the precautions that you have to take to prevent the constant password stealing problems from taking place are relatively simple. In this book, you will learn a lot about how you can come up with strong passwords. Also included in this book are some of the supporting pieces of information that can help you raise awareness on why you have to come up with strong passwords in the first place.

There are numerous benefits that you can acquire just by staying informed. For one thing, reading the book can help you develop your enhanced sense of guarding your accounts against potential threats. Also, you can help the people that you care about save their accounts from risks of online identity theft as well.

Table of Contents

Introduction/Overview

Providing computer security can be trickier than you think. With this in mind, you need to learn some guidelines to help you proportionally improve your security not only for your computer but also for your online accounts. Specifically, in this guidance you will learn more on how you can come up with stronger passwords for your account(s).

There are certain things that you have to observe when creating your passwords for your accounts.

First, you need to use at least five characters. Using a password with less than five characters can make it much easier for the hackers to access your account. To help further reinforce the security levels of your account, you have to use a combination of lower case and upper case of letters. You may also add symbols and numbers to your password.

On the other hand, you should not use any form of private information that can relate to your identity. In other words, you should not use birthdates, the maiden name of your mother, social security numbers, phone numbers, e-mail addresses, residential addresses, and your own name. These pieces of information are relatively easy to guess. Therefore, potential hackers will find it easier to access your accounts without you knowing it.

In line with the previous point, you may employ ways on how to devise effective and long passwords that you can still remember no matter what.

You may use a fun sentence that you can definitely remember. Sports teams, movie titles, book titles, and favorite song titles will also work. After this, you may select the first or the first two letters. Changing some of the letters of these choices into symbols can also help a lot. For websites that encourage the use of case sensitive passwords, you may use a varying combination of lower case and upper case letters.

You also have to observe some safety guidelines in composing your password.

First, you should not share your password except with your parents or an adult that you fully trust. For every online account that you own, you should also use a different type of password. This is regardless of the nature of the account that you will be using. As much as possible, you should also make it a point to change your password. Experts recommend you to change your online account passwords every six months.

Chapter 1: What Are Digital Footprints?

Digital footprint is a term used to describe the traces or the trail of online footprints that people tend to leave on different sites. These are pieces of information that are transmitted through different online sites. There are numerous pieces of information that may be transmitted online. Some of these include digital images, video clips, electronic mail attachments, and forum registration. In the long run, these things leave lots of traces of personalized information about you. These things are made available to people who go online.

There is some probability that you do not regard your digital footprint with much importance as of this moment.

However, you should realize that this is more important than you think. Your personal digital footprint may also refer to the type of reputation that you have established online. Aside from this, your visibility is revealed when as person searches for pieces of information about you on the web.

There are numerous forms of online visibility in social media sites. This may include some of the following: photos of you and your friends in a party, video of your latest presentations with your colleagues, and an article that mentions you and your loved ones. Actually, the possibilities are endless. Depending on the settings placed for online visibility, anyone who performs assessment can see these contents online.

In the realm of retail and banking sites, digital footprints can significantly affect the creation of economic value of a certain institution.

A part of the generated GDP in the virtual realm can continue to increase or decrease depending on the online reputation that a certain institution has established as of the moment. Also, there may be the emergence of compensation models and new revenues that can reward your ability to influence and sense the intentions of other people before they may be translated into action. In this regard, institutions can use the digital footprints to proactively address the issues and needs of their clients. Using digital footprints, they can have the ability to help other groups or companies in expanding their influence and businesses in the realm of social media.

Chapter 2: Reasons for not Storing Your Password in a Browser

Recalling your passwords for different websites can be extremely annoying. Given this premise, it is still not a good idea for you to allow your web browser to do this task for you.

Software developers have noted that it is extremely easy for an amateur to view the passwords that you have stored in your browser.

This is provided that you have used a personal computer unit that they also have access to. Basically, the person simply has to go to the settings of the browser concerned and locate the list of passwords stored in it. After this, all you have to do is to click the "show" command on these passwords so you can see it in plain view. Given the fact that it is relatively easy to do this by anyone armed with the correct knowledge, you have to be aware of the amount of data that you may be exposing the moment that you sign in using your preferred web browser. This concern becomes increasingly important because most of the web browsers do not require generic prompts or master passwords just before you gain access to the passwords stored in the browser.

The main problem that most experts raise is the fact that most clients do not expect the possibility of extremely easy access to their personal data.

This drives them to address the developers of these web browsers to clarify their security policies. This will help the browser users come up with a more informed decision. Another suggestion that the developers gave is the possibility of adding an option to add a master password before the users can view the other passwords used in different websites.

The most secure method to store sensitive pieces of information like this is to avoid storing your passwords in your browser.

Aside from the minimal available security options for you, there are also a lot of host for possible threats that are lurking online. In other words, other online users may gain access to your passwords even if they do not have access to your personal computer unit. Therefore, the best way is to keep it in your memory if possible.

Chapter 3: Reasons to Create Numerous Passwords

It is definitely a difficult task to track the number of passwords and usernames or IDs that you have for different applications and Internet sites. For starters, it is important to have different passwords for your software and online accounts because having only a few of them can make it easier for other people to access all of your accounts once one of them has been discovered. In this book section are some of the insights regarding having multiple unique passwords for numerous accounts.

You need to have numerous passwords to help you in significantly decreasing the possibility of being hacked in the future.

You should especially provide different passwords for "sensitive accounts". Some examples of these accounts include the following: social media site accounts, online bank accounts, and website management accounts.

Having numerous passwords at the ready can help discourage the potential hackers from dwelling too much on how to hack your system.

Because they have a hard time getting anything vital from your accounts, they will eventually get tired of doing that and will leave your accounts to simply search for others that they can gain access to more readily.

Some people devise different means to recall their passwords effectively despite the fact that there are too many of them.

Experts advise you to write down your credentials and keep them close to you as much as possible. Apparently, this is not considered as the safest way to deal with too many passwords but it can somehow aid with the recall part.

To help you prioritize which password to remember, you have to determine the websites that you consider as important for you.

You may list down at least five or six of these sites. After doing so, you should make sure that the passwords that you will create are all hard to guess and unique passwords for each of them. These should not be related to each other as well. In this regard, one way to help you remember the passwords is to come up with a picture that can help somehow associate these passwords with each other without other people noticing the connection.

Chapter 4: How to Create a Strong Password

Account passwords are essential for proper online management because they help protect your accounts from unauthorized online use. In this regard, you have to make sure that you will compose highly secured passwords for your accounts. In the long run, this can help protect vital pieces of information from being stolen.

There are some things that you can do to help you come up with the best passwords.

First off, you need to choose a password that you will definitely remember as much as possible. You also have to change this regularly. Additionally, you have to use a type of password that you can quickly type without looking at the keyboard. It will be relatively difficult for the other people to see what you are typing even when they look over your shoulders.

As much as possible, you should use a password with at least eight characters. If you can add more to the word count, you have to do this by all means. This will further help in boosting your password's security capability.

On the other hand, there are also things that you have to avoid doing so you can come up with safe passwords.

For starters, you should never select your username to act as your password as well. Also, you are not to share your password with anyone that you have just met. Once you do, you will never know who can gain access to your password.

You should not use easily predictable alphabet sequences or number sequences. You are even discouraged to use keyboard sequences because password hacking applications can easily decipher these patterns. Therefore, it will only take a while before the hackers get access to your accounts using your passwords.

Moreover, you are discouraged from a word that has been spelled backwards as your password. If you are using a password with the same letters or numbers for the entire length, you are in for a great risk of account hacking. You are also discouraged from substituting numbers to act as letters for your passwords. More of the dictionary applications have a way of going around this password generation trick.

Chapter 5: How Passwords Are Stolen

There are many ways that a password may be stolen by hackers. Most of them rely on tools such as sniffers and dictionary programs to help crack the much wanted codes. In this book section, you will learn more about how they do this. Having a good idea on how they perform the act can help you prevent your account from being hacked altogether.

It may take some time for the hackers to crack your password using sniffers and dictionary based applications but they can finish off faster if you have a relatively easy password.

Hackers will launch their dictionary based attacks by trying out every word that they can find in the dictionary. This dictionary also contains foreign languages and English phrases. This application is connected to a login program. The main focus of this attack is to eventually find out the password through "manual means".

Sniffers work by "reading" the key strokes that you make while using your personal computer unit or other similar devices. This may or may not include the encoding of passwords in their respective fields.

Phising may also be used as a means to obtain your password. This is a method that prompts a user to enter their login ID and password in a website. This is typically fronted by the guise that their password may be compromised.

Interestingly, a large percentage of stolen passwords are mainly because of the users' fault.

Some of the users willingly share passwords when they are asked to do so. More importantly, they can be very predictable when it comes to the personal choice of their passwords. Some may even come up with passwords that are too short. Therefore, this makes it easy for the hackers to guess what their passwords are. Sometimes, the identities of the users are readily reflected in their passwords. In the hopes of avoiding dictionary attacks, some even resort to the use of obscure foreign words because they think that these will not be identified by the dictionary software. To sum it up, these passwords can all be easily guessed. This makes hacking straightforward.

Chapter 6: Defining Hashes and Rainbow Tables

Knowing more about hashes and rainbow tables can help you be more familiar in the art of password hacking. Raising awareness about these things can help you be more proactive in protecting your accounts and yourself against online identity theft. This book section can tell you more about these two things.

A hash is also known as a checksum or a digest.

This is considered as a type of signature intended for streams of data. The streams of data represent the content. In this regard, the closest reality based analogue is a seal in an application package. This software package has a seal that is usually tamper evident. If you can change the file by opening the box, this can be detected.

Numerous Linux and Unix systems can provide md5sum programs. These programs can produce a 128 bit fixed number and a stream of data. These things can help summarize the stream of data by utilizing the famous MD5 procedure. In this regard, the files are considered as streams of data. There are two versions of files that you can directly view. On the other hand, there is just one that is typically too large for display. You can see the avalanche effect if you view hashes with similar lengths.

There are numerous mechanisms that can make rainbow tables work.

The main component that can help you understand the rainbow tables is to fully comprehend the reduction function. Usually, hash functions are used to map the plaintexts to the hashes. On the other hand, the reduction functions help map the hashes to the plaintexts.

It is essential to note that the latter typically performs the reverse function of hash functions. However, this is not considered as the inverse of hash functions. The whole point of having hash functions is the probability that the inverse hash functions cannot be created. If you take out the hash of a certain plaintext and eventually take out the hash reduction, this will not yield you with the original plaintext. In the long run, this will only give you another type of plaintext.

Hashes are considered as one way functions. This goes the same for the reduction functions. The chains that eventually make up the rainbow tables the chains of reduction functions and one way hash functions.

Chapter 7: Why Password Security Should Be Prioritized

Think of this analogy, your account password is highly similar to your house key. This can help keep out the unwanted intruders and guests. Leaving an unprotected password is highly comparable to the act of leaving your house key at your doorstep. A person who guesses or steals your account password from you can use this to obtain unauthorized access to computer accounts, files, electronic mail, and your identity.

Usually, hackers use the stolen passwords in covering their tracks when they perform online crimes like fraud.

Other online crimes that they may perform include the following: breaking into other online systems, making threats, spamming, and child pornography. If they have used your account and password for these purposes, the immediate evidence will be directly pointed toward your computer account.

Even if you can trust all the people in your immediate environment, there is a chance that anyone can obtain your user ID and password for a certain account.

If your computer system has been connected to the Internet, anyone who has capability to connect using this method can also try accessing your accounts by guessing the account's password. All that they need to obtain is your ID or account name. Relatively, this type of information is not hard to extract from numerous computer systems.

As soon as an online intruder acquires your password, they can readily access and modify any piece of information that you store in your account.

They can even access and change the accounts of the people on your system if the website allows this function. Moreover, they can use your account to break into other types of systems as well. They can use this to exploit other types of security holes in your operating system. Ultimately, they can use the account to break in the system that can provide easy access to all of the accounts found in a certain system. Given these premises, an online intruder will only require you to compromise at least one account found in the system. After this, they can freely attack the "supervisor accounts". This will help them access the entire system where your account is directly or indirectly involved.

Chapter 8: How Hackers Obtain and Use Passwords

There are numerous corporate guidelines to date. However, they do not really assist people in choosing the passwords that they should come up with to prevent the risks of having their accounts hacked. As in many security related places, there is a disconnection that exists between the manner that people secure their systems and the methods that hackers employ to break these systems. This book section will tell you something about what the hackers can do with your passwords and how they crack these seemingly elusive codes.

Hackers will perform a lot of word and phrase mutations in an attempt to obtain your account password.

This point makes the creation of long passwords so important. If you have a password with at least eight characters, they will have a relatively hard time looking that up in their dictionary. The difficulty level is heightened even more if you choose an insane combination of letters, numbers, symbols, and capitalizations. The following is a list of typical mutations that hackers may try on most dictionary words:

- Place spaces or punctuation marks between each word

- Mix two words together

- Duplicate all the letters of a word

- Duplicate the first letter of a word

- Place punctuation marks at the end of the words

- Replace the letters "I" and "O" with the numbers "1" and "0", respectively

- Place the same type of pattern for both ends

- Insert some numbers at the beginning of the words

- Type in some numbers at the end of the words

- Insert a random number in a word

- Check all combinations of lowercase or uppercase for words

- Capitalize first letters of words

One of the most common concerns is the online versus offline attacks.

An online attack is the instance that the hacker attempts to log in and pretends to be the owner of your account. Typically, they try to guess your password. Unless you have selected something that is relatively easy to guess, this may not be considered as an immediate danger. Usually, the online system will automatically lock your account once "you" have made too many incorrect password guesses.

On the other hand, offline password cracking is considered as the real danger. For this approach, the hacker will break into a system. The hacker will do this to eavesdrop on the encrypted exchange on the Internet. They may also do this to obtain the encrypted password file. After this, they are eventually free to perform password decrypting without anyone stopping their acts. For this method, they can guess passwords with a rate of approximately one billion guesses in a second.

Chapter 9: Knowing More About Password Managers

A password manager is considered as a type of application that can aid you in organizing your PIN codes and passwords. Usually, the application possesses a file or a local database that can hold encrypted password data. This is done to enable secure log-ins in application data files, websites, networks, and computers. Most of the password managers also serve as form fillers. In this regard, they are used to automatically fill out the password and user ID data in online forms. You can implement this using USB stick applications, smart card applications, and browser extensions. These tools can help communicate to your browser or other related applications.

These password managers can come in numerous variations.

The variations are classified according to the medium used so you can gain access to them. The software developers may combine some of these variations. This is usually done to create a more effective password manager for you.

- For stateless types, you can generate the passwords on the fly. This means that you have to create the password from master pass phrases and tags that utilize key derivation functions.

- Cloud based online password managers are avenues where you can readily store credentials. Specifically, the credentials are stored in the servers of the service providers. These servers are found on the Internet. However, the password management application handles this while it runs on the machine of the user.

- On the other hand, web based online password managers can help you readily see your passwords. These password managers can also help you copy the passwords to and from the website of the provider.

- Token password managers have credentials that are protected through security tokens. Therefore, they can usually offer you multi-factor authentication. Protection is reinforced through the combination of USB sticks or smart cards. Additionally, passwords or PINs are also used. For advanced systems, biometrics may also be employed. This is done to further boost the security levels for the user's account.

- Portable application storing programs and passwords found on mobile equipment may be used to manage your passwords. Some of these include the following: USB memory sticks, portable applications, smart phones, and PDAs (personal digit assistants).

- Laptop or desktop application storing passwords may be users for computer hard drives.

One of the most apparent advantages of the password based access controls is the fact that you can easily incorporate them in most types of applications that use APIs.

These APIs are typically available in numerous software products. They do not need extensive server or computer modifications. Also, you are most likely familiar with account password use already so you will not have a hard time using this. While most of the passwords, may be considered fairly secure, there may be a problem in managing and choosing them. It is quite usual to commit at least one of the password related mistakes.

You may use password managers to help defend your account against pharming and phising.

Phising has been briefly discussed in a previous chapter. On the other hand, pharming is a form of cyber attack that aims to redirect the traffic of a certain website to a bogus website. Unlike humans, password manager applications can incorporate automated log-in scripts. These scripts initially compare the URL of the current website to the URL of the stored website. If these two do not match, then the application will not fill out the log-in fields automatically. This move intends to act as a form of safeguard against look-alike sites and other forms of online visual imitations.

Because of this built-in advantage, using a password manager can be beneficial. This is considered beneficial even if you only have a few passwords that you need to recall. While not all types of password managers can handle complex log-in methods automatically, most of the latest ones can help do this for you.

Browser based and desktop type password managers are considered as convenient tools.

However, they usually do not provide you with any form of protection for your stored passwords. If you have turned on your personal computer unit, it is probable for another person to gain access to the password manager. This person can read your password as well if they know how to use the software. You can slightly improve the situation by tweaking the settings of the application in such a way that they will require the current user to type in the password. This password will be used to gain access to the repository. This password and the rest of your passwords should be encrypted at all times.

Chapter 10: On Browser Based and Online Password Managers

All types of password managers are typically designed to help significantly reduce the burden of recalling numerous unique passwords at the same time. This is considered as a necessity if you are aiming to minimize the online security risks that you may encounter along the way. There are numerous password managers to choose from. This includes the password saving features of your built-in browsers. There are two main types of password managers. These are the online and the desktop varieties. This book section will inform you about the pros and cons of using some specific password managers. This part of the book can somehow guide you in choosing an application that can best suit your needs.

Some of the online password managers are Dashlane, LastPass, and 1Password.

Android, iPhone, Mac, and Windows can adequately support the use of Dashlane. This is a free password manager. Some of its unique features include the following: can save receipts, presence of security alerts, quick auditing of passwords that are not secured, and the ability to turn off cloud sync when needed. In terms of security features, this has a 256 bit AES. Also included is a disable or selective sync. You have to pay the premium version on a monthly or yearly basis. Doing so will enable this application to help you add more secure notes. The premium version can also provide you with more mobile applications.

LastPass is supported by operating systems like Android, iPad, iPhone, premium plan supports, Linux, Mac, Windows Phone, BlackBerry and Windows. This is also a free application. For this password manager, you only have to enter your password once. This is also embedded with security audits and alerts. You can use multiple online accounts of different people for this application. Secure sharing is allowed. Credit monitoring is possible with this software as well. This has a 256 bit AES. You can readily view a security history once you use this application. The security history typically consists of log-ins tracking and events tracking. The system will also prompt you to have a two factor authentication. To help prevent the risks of keystroke identification, the application is equipped with a screen keyboard log-in. This password manager has a premium version that you can pay on an annual basis. The premium version can readily support multifactor authentication through USB thumb drives. Yubikeys can also work. No ads are present while using this software. Also, this can provide you with mobile applications.

Windows Phone 7, Android, iPad, iPhone, Mac, and Windows platforms can support the use of 1Password. Unlike the first two password managers, you have to shell out around $50 so you can obtain this software. You may use the 1PasswordAnywhere feature to see your data files from storage sites such as external drives. You may use Dropbox as an optional cross platform for data sync processes. If you have previously saved bookmarks, you may use this to perform one click log-ins. Automatic backups are also possible for this application. This has a 128 bit AES. Moreover, this password manager can clear up the clipboard values after a predetermined period of time. Additionally, the developers provide you with a one month trial period. You can also avail bundle licenses. You may even purchase iOS applications for a better experience in password management.

On the other hand, SplashID, Roboform, and KeePass are some good examples of desktop password managers.

Windows Phone, BlackBerry, Android, iPad, iPhone, Linux, and Windows platforms may be used to activate KeePass. This password manager is free. Some of its unique features include the following: numerous plug-ins, ability to sync on local networks, efficient simultaneous handling of multiple users, convenience, and its open source nature. This has a Twofish and AES algorithm support. Moreover, the 256 bit or SHA-256 password hash can help manage your passwords even better. While this application is running, the passwords will remain encrypted. As for password editing, you can enjoy a security enhanced interface. Instead of having a master password for added security, this password manager utilizes key files.

Windows is Roboform's chosen platform. You can purchase this password manager for approximately $30. There is a portable variation of this software. One of the features that set this apart from the other password managers is the fact that you can perform secure sharing. Multiple user support is also a unique feature that this software boasts of. As for the security features of this password manager, this also has a screen keyboard log-in feature. The algorithm is an AES 256 bit. Roboform

Everywhere is the cloud syncing version of this password manager. The trial version provides you with free access for 10 log-ins. If you are satisfied with this version, you may purchase this for around $10 a year. This will grant you unlimited access.

SplashID permits the use of platforms like Windows Phone, Android, iPad, iPhone, Max, and Windows. You can obtain this password manager for approximately $20. One of its unique features is the de-dupe tool. This application is also equipped with reminders. These can help you recall the passwords that you have to change already. Secure sharing is also available for this password manager. Moreover, this is equipped with a password tracing feature if you are using this on your touchscreen device. Blowfish cipher or AES 256 bit is a security feature of this software. You may purchase its mobile applications for around $10.

Chapter 11: Essential Features of Password Management Systems

Given the number of various sets of online credentials for log-in that you need, the management of strong passwords can seem like a great challenge for you. This is one of the main reasons that you need to use one or more password managers. To help you choose the right type of password manager for you, this book section will present you with some of the most important features that you have to look out for in a password management system.

The stored log-in credentials must be stored in encrypted form.

You are advised to use strong and heavily tested encryptions. These should be peer reviewed as well. This will help you recover your account from the online thief. This is possible because the hacker cannot recover the stolen password once you use your password manager.

A good password management system should also greatly consider the unlocked screens.

Believe it or not, there are some people who temporarily leave their work stations with the screens of their devices unlocked easily accessible by a potential hacker. It is essential that the system will automatically log out the user after a given period of time. This should be the case if the device has been idle for too long. Moreover, this system should be able to effectively hide the passwords on your screen after a given period of time. Also, the virtual clipboards of your workstation should be kept clear automatically if the passwords have been copied to it.

Password synchronization is also a must for this type of system.

Password synchronization is considered as any kind of technology or process that can help you maintain a password across multiple systems. This password is subject to the single security policy. This feature is regarded as an efficient and effective mechanism that you can use to address problems related to password management.

- Users who have synchronized password have the tendency to recall their passwords.

- The simpler password management systems imply that users like you tend to make fewer calls to the help desk regarding the password related concerns.

- Also, users who only own one or two passwords have a greater probability of writing down their passwords.

Self contained functionality is another feature of these systems.

Numerous applications for password management are not readily written with your absolute data security in mind. However, this does not mean that applications like these do not trust the security levels that the external applications can provide. While these systems contain most of the password storing and protecting functionalities, it will do little to boost these systems to help them further do their jobs in the long run.

Chapter 12: Examining the Master Passphrase

The master passphrase feature will permit you to securely perform storage for plain text passwords. The storage procedure is done in encrypted format. This feature can give you a key that you may use to universally mask or encrypt all of your passwords. This is done without changing any of the functionalities of your password management system.

There are some password types that can take advantage of this type of feature.

These passwords include the following:

- Shared licenses
- Logging
- AAA servers
- Failover
- Site to site and remote access VPN
- Load balancing VPN
- EIGRP
- OSPF

There are some prerequisites before you can effectively use the master passphrase feature.

If the failover has been enabled but there is no set failover shared key, then modifying the master passphrase will display an error message. The error message will inform you that you have to enter a failover shared key. This will help protect the changes of the master passphrase from being sent out in the form of plain text. This method will only be allowed if your settings enable you to have a secure session. Some of the means that you have to use are the following: through HTTPS, ASDM, SSH, and console.

Chapter 13: Pros and Cons of Password Management Software

Password managers are known for their ability to help you in significantly reducing the burden of remembering passwords for your online accounts. Because you need not worry much about the recall part, all you have to do is to create strong sets of passwords that hackers cannot easily hack in the long run.

Aside from these, there are lots of pros that password managers can provide you.

For one thing, password managers have a good balance of security and convenience. Even if you create passwords that are too complicated to type in everytime you log in, you do not have to worry because these applications can readily fill out the password portion of the online forms. This can also come in handy when you have to answer secret questions that you provided for your online accounts.

In relation to the previous point, you can also use your password managers not just for passwords but also for pieces of vital information like passport numbers, credit card numbers, insurance numbers, and bank details. They can be readily stored in the application.

Secure storage is possible because the sensitive pieces of information will be encrypted as soon as they are placed in the system's storage. This is then protected using a master password. Compared to the traditional means of writing down the password elsewhere, this is considered a lot better. This is also a better choice than encoding your password in an unencrypted spreadsheet or note.

Also included are some of the cons that you may encounter along the way while using these password managers.

If you fail in one aspect of password safekeeping, all your passwords and accounts may be gone for good. For instance, if you sync the key to your personal computer unit or your phone, some people may gain some access to that.

Trusting in the cloud is another downside of password managers. For password related data, they should be encrypted in storage. However, if you perform data synchronization, this may make you end up having a disgruntled or malicious employee access.

Chapter 14: Free Password Managers

Maintaining a relatively large assortment of unique and strong passwords is often considered as a challenge. In this book section, you will learn more about some of the password management applications. These applications can help make your maintenance job a lot easier than before.

Clipperz is an online password management website that can help you closely monitor all of your passwords.

This can store your entries in the form of cards. You may create the cards for direct log-in, custom, bank accounts, and for web purposes. This site can also provide you with a Compact edition. This version can work as a sidebar for some of your browsers.

Passpack is another type of online password manager that can offer you both paid and free accounts.

This online password manager has been around for a long time. In fact, this is already recommended by large companies. The free version limits the amount of passwords that you are allowed to keep in the system's database. Aside from the basic features, this has a unique feature known as the Passpack It! option. This permits you to perform one click entries into numerous sites that require authentication.

KeePassX is a kind of open source cross platform tool that can offer you extensive password management features.

The platform tool will enable you to search in the complete database or in specific groups. This highly depends on the search related options that you have specified before you performed the actual search. You may access the system's database by using a key file or a password.

Password Gorilla is considered as a simple type of cross platform application that assists in log-in management.

This can store miscellaneous notes, log-in information, passwords, and user names in securely encrypted files. In typical fashion, one master password is used to help you protect the encrypted file. This encrypted file contains the database of the password. Aside from this, there are really nothing spectacular about this application.

Chapter 15: Future Biometric Alternatives

Biometrics closely refers to metrics or quantifiable data that are highly related to the human traits and characteristics. This is typically used for access control and identification. In this book section, you will learn more about some of the alternatives to passwords that you can definitely gain a lot of benefit from.

The electrical signals and activity of your heart are very difficult to replicate.

One of the main reasons behind this is the fact that heartbeats are distinct. Identification of ECG (electrocardiograph) signals is possible now regardless of where you are because of the recent technological advancements. For instance, Apple's iPhone is already equipped with an embedded feature that allows you to monitor your heart rate readily. In the long run, this may be used for account ownership identification.

Sensitive touchscreens can already make out the shape of your ear readily.

At present, this is an idea designed for the Ergo Android app. When you press your ear against the screen of the device, the points of contact of the ear surface with the glass are initially mapped out. This is then compared to the baseline print of the "stored ear". You will be authenticated to gain access to the device and/or account if these two inputs match.

Similar to fingerprints, face recognition is already used in some devices.

Your device needs to have a sharp and clear image to begin with. For this purpose, the built-in cameras found in the tablets and smartphones are usually sufficient.

Conclusion

It is extremely important for you to thoroughly know and understand more about proper password management and what to use so you can safeguard your accounts against unauthorized use. In the long run, these pieces of information can help you prevent problems that may arise because of negligence to follow relatively simple guidelines that you have to take note of everytime you are required to create a strong password for your account.

After reading this book, you are expected to have gained the ability to apply what you have learned in creating stronger passwords for your accounts in the future. You should also use the information to help you significantly decrease your risks of falling prey to online identity thieves.

Book Review

Thank you for reading my *book Your Digital Footprint Password Protection Requirements.* If you ever have a spare moment, it would be a great help if you could post a review of it on Amazon and let other potential readers know why you liked it. It's not necessary to write a lengthy, formal review—a summary of the comments from you would be perfectly fine. Here's a link to the review form for my book:

About the Author

Ronald has been writing as a hobby for over twenty years. He has completed a collection of multiple genres in both fiction and nonfiction that include financial, estate, cooking and identity theft. In the area of fiction he has published humor, science fiction, romance and fantasy. He is polishing up some children's, paranormal romance, erotica romance and additional science fiction books. He has approximately 50 additional plot outlines completed and their associated books in various stages of completion. We can anticipate more stories in the areas of finance, children's and young adult reading as well as humor, fantasy, romance, thrillers and even some mystery and steampunk. Only the author's files and mind know the definitive creations yet to be.

Ronald E. Hudkins (1951-Present) now residing in Durango, Colorado was born in Canton, Ohio and raised in Massillon, Ohio. He was drafted into military service in 1970 where he remained up until 1993 when he retired honorably from the U.S. Army, Military Police Corps. During his service, after and in between a lot of traveling he attended many universities that include Kent State University, Maryland University, Central Texas College (European Branch), Blair Junior College, Hagerstown Junior College and Phoenix University. He declared two majors in the areas of Business Administration and a Bachelor of Science in Information Technology.

To learn more about this author visit his author platform at

Additional Reading

 Fiction – Humor - Titled **Senior Things I Said, Say, Did and Do.** Publication Date: Dec 21 2012, ASIN: B00GB5NL36, ISBN-10: 1481174452, ISBN-13: 978-1481174459, EBook ISBN9781310746864. Page Count: 190. Available in paperback, eReader and eBook formats.

 Fiction – Humor - Titled **The Summer of Lost Soles**. Publication Date: March 20, 2013, ASIN: B00GB5MEAC, ISBN-10: 148392503X, ISBN-13: 978-1483925035, EBook ISBN 9781310442438. Page Count 126. Available in paperback, eReader, eBook and Audio formats.

 Fiction – Science Fiction - Titled **The Thirty Century War**. Publication Date: November 16, 2013, ASIN: B00GQBYX8M, ISBN-13: 978-1493780501, ISBN-10: 1493780506, EBook ISBN

781310233098. Page Count 46.   Available in paperback, eReader and eBook formats.

 Fiction – Fantasy – Titled **The Cape Coral Heroes**. Publication Date: March 19, 2014, ASIN: B00JDMNCWE, ISBN-13: 978-1497398528, ISBN-10: 1497398525, EBook ISBN: 9781310916489. Page Count 106. Available in paperback, eReader and eBook formats.

 Nonfiction – Financial – Titled **Basic, Savings and Checking Account Guidance: for Teens and Young Adults**. Publication Date: March 7, 2014, ASIN: B00J1O3CEC, ISBN-13: 978-1496198273, ISBN-10: 1496198271, EBook ISBN: 9781311044891. Page Count 172. Available in paperback, eReader and eBook formats.

Nonfiction – Medical Reference and Cookbook – Titled **What Makes Cannabis Recipes Work?** Publication Date: Dec 26 2013 ASIN: BOOHJB4KNG, ISBN: 1494796104, EAN13: 9781494796105, EBook ISBN 9781311324115. Page Count 46. Available in paperback, eReader and eBook formats.

You can get these two Ebooks Titled **How to Avoid Identity Theft** and **Asset Protection and Estate Planning for All Ages** just by visiting the author's website. Two subject areas that are a must read for every adult concerned about their financial integrity.

Internet Presence Ronald Hudkins

My Other Projects page is where friends and followers of the author Ronald E. Hudkins and publisher of the book Senior Things I Said, Say, Did and Do Volume One can see the authors other Internet activities.

Business Sites on the Internet

The Healthy Living Mall

Ever just want a one source stop for Diet and Weight loss, Exercise and Fitness, Mental Health, Men's Health, Nutrition and Women's Health? That storefront is now here! Visit http://digijunction.com/health/guard1

What is The Healthy Living Mall?

The healthy living mall is unlike any other place you have visited before. I am sure you care about your health more than anyone else in the world and the healthy living mall is the one place that can help you. The healthy living mall is like a library that has the knowledge, expertise, and experience to help you achieve your health goals.

Do not worry about what your overall goal is because the healthy living mall has what you need. Some of you may have a goal to lose weight or improve fitness. Some of you may even be trying to focus on one specific aspect on your health.

These are all noble goals and this site can help you achieve any of them that you chose to work on.

Now you do not have to have a goal to work out every day or get ripped. Part of why this site is here for everyone is because it helps people work with conventional treatments as well as other non-traditional methods. Some people prefer more natural and alternative medicines which work just as well. The healthy living mall gives you this power over your health and gives you the knowledge to make these important decisions.

The way this site works is by breaking down all your possible needs into different sections. This makes it much easier for you to navigate your way through and easily find everything you need. All the information here is free for you so be sure to take advantage of it whenever you want.

The Health Mall is constantly being updated with the newest and latest health information. You should go ahead and save this page to your favorites and your bookmarks. This way you can easily get here again later. So, check us out at **http://digijunction.com/health/guard1**

Home Business Resource Center

If there is anything you need to know about Affiliate Marketing, Auctions, Classified Ads, Consulting, Home Employment, Internet Marketing, Paid Surveys or Software this is your home business resource, training and most up to date news information available to date on the Internet!
Visit;**http://digijunction.com/business/guard1**

About the ultimate Home Business Resource Center.

Maybe you are looking for a little extra cash. Or maybe you'd like to tell your boss that he can "take your job and give it to some other sucker". Whatever your reason for looking for a new home based business you've come to the right place.

With all the scams and downright bogus products out there it can be hard to decipher the legitimate opportunities from the duds. Well, we've made it extremely easy for you by providing you with access to the very best programs in the entire home based business categories. Look at this site as your perfect one stop shop for finding your perfect home business.

Perhaps you are looking for a home business that can replace a full time income or even produce a six or seven figure income. While some of you might be looking to pocket an extra few hundred to a few thousand dollars in your spare time. Whichever category you fall under this site will have the perfect business for you.

This site is broken down into several categories to help you find what is right for you. Whether you are a beginner or a seasoned pro you'll be sure to find the perfect home business here.

So go ahead, look around and find the home business that is right for you.

Also, please be sure to bookmark this site as we make updates with the newest and hottest programs often.

http://digijunction.com/business/guard1

Investing for Profit

If you are looking for some of the very best investment programs and services relative to Commodities, Forex, Options, Personal Finance, Real Estate and Stocks this site has you covered. Remember, the right knowledge can mean the difference between significant gains and catastrophic losses. We're here to give you the right knowledge for each market. Visit; http://digijunction.com/investing/guard1

About Investing for Profit

If you are guessing or simply do not know what you are doing in the world of investment you can lose a lot of your hard earned money. Sure, you can get lucky and actually establish some profitable investments but you can also see your profits get wiped out in an instant. However with the proper guidance, tools and self help education you can learn to limit any losses in any market and this site is designed specifically to show you how.

Here at the Investing for Profit digital mall you will find the absolute top of the line investment programs and service that are currently or about to be available. It does not matter where you interests are held be it in Stocks, FOREX, options, real estate or stocks this site will keep you investing intelligently. You know as well as I the difference between exceptional gains or disastrous losses boils down to just having the correct knowledge. At this site you have the complete and correct knowledge no matter which market you invest in.

One of the best things about the Investing for Profit Mall is the selection of programs that are available. Different sectors and trading styles can be hot at various times. When there is a bull market in natural gas, gold or oil you can check out the many featured programs in the commodities trading area. If the stock market is sinking maybe with more investment option programs is right for you. This site allows you to educate yourself completely for whatever market you choose to place your investments.

So go ahead, look around and find the investing strategies that are right for you. Also, please be sure to bookmark this site as we make updates with the newest and hottest programs often.

http://digijunction.com/investing/guard1

StoreDoor

StoreDoor is a place where the mugs are just a little bit different. Perhaps a bit bitter/sweet for the person looking for a slightly different (not so tactful) way to express a crude feeling about a person, place, thing or event.

http://www.zazzle.com/storedoor

Member Social Sites

Delicious.com (Article Postings)

http://www.delicious.com/stacks/view/EkApbc

Stumbpleupon.com

http://www.stumbleupon.com/stumbler/ron29950

Digg.com (Article Postings)

http://digg.com/settings/links

YouTube

http://www.youtube.com/user/rh112131

Pinterest

http://www.pinterest.com/rhudkins/

Facebook (Follow Me!)

https://www.facebook.com/ronald.hudkins

Twitter

https://twitter.com/HudkinsR

Figment

http://figment.com/users/361031-Ronald-E-Hudkins

Wattpad

http://www.wattpad.com/user/rhudkinsv

Goodreads

https://www.goodreads.com/user/show/158 53675-ronald-hudkins

Amazon Page

http://www.amazon.com/-/e/B00ATQ83JA

Shelfari

http://www.shelfari.com/ronaldhudkins

Linkedin

http://www.linkedin.com/pub/ronald-hudkins/4a/356/749

Smashwords

https://www.smashwords.com/profile/view/r hudkins **ask David**

http://askdavid.com/books/7702

Public Bio's

Expert Author Bio on EzineArticles

http://ezinearticles.com/?expert=Ronald_Hu dkins

Linkedin.com (Business Profile Page)

http://www.linkedin.com/pub/ronald-hudkins/4a/356/749

MarketerProfiles.com (by Charlie Page)

http://www.marketerprofiles.com/?a=h&c=&mode=&p=4

 Blog Spots on the Internet

SelfGrowth.com

http://www.selfgrowth.com/experts/ronald_hudkins.html

Slide Shows

Slide Presentations -
http://www.slideshare.net/hudkinsr

Author Stream - Video Presentations

http://www.authorstream.com/Presentation/aSGuest130361-1369066-10-slightly-different-ways-to-advertise/

www.ingramcontent.com/pod-product-compliance
Lightning Source LLC
Chambersburg PA
CBHW061033050326
40689CB00012B/2807